Exploring with the
LEWIS AND CLARK
EXPEDITION

A This or That Debate

by Jessica Rusick

CAPSTONE PRESS
a capstone imprint

Capstone Captivate is published by Capstone Press, an imprint of Capstone.
1710 Roe Crest Drive
North Mankato, Minnesota 56003
www.capstonepub.com

Library of Congress Cataloging-in-Publication Data is available on the Library of Congress website.
ISBN: 978-1-4966-8389-2 (library binding)
ISBN: 978-1-4966-8787-6 (paperback)
ISBN: 978-1-4966-8440-0 (eBook PDF)

Summary: In 1804, the Lewis & Clark Expedition set out to explore new U.S. land west of the Mississippi River. Test your decision-making skills with this or that questions related to their quest!

Image Credits
Alamy: Pictorial Press Ltd, 5; Discovering Lewis & Clark: © 2018 by Kristopher Townsend. Used by permission. Portable soup created by JohnFisher, 22; Flickr: BLMIdaho, 16, F Delventhal, 12, Forest Service Northern Region, 3, Goffres, 25 (surgical manual), Internet Archive Book Images, 13; iStockphoto: boblin, 20; Shutterstock Images: bddigitalimages, 24 (medical supplies), Bilanol, 26, Doin, Cover (canoe), Eileen McSherry, 27, Eric Isselee, 30, Everett Historical, Cover (map), 6 (map), 7 (map), 9, 32, Goran Bogicevic, Cover (paddle), Igor Shoshin, 14, Joseph Sohm, Cover (landscape), 18, Ken Schulze, Cover (military cap), Leigh Anne Meeks, 17, Leremy, 24, 25, Maksimilian, 11, Michael Warwick, 19, Petr Malyshev, Cover (fur hat), tavizta, 15, Thye-Wee Gn, Cover (Fort Clatsop), Tristan Brynildsen, 29, Zoran Milic, 5 (map); U.S. National Park Service: Richard Schlecht/Richard Schlecht Illustrations, 8, Tom Kozar, 6 (Lewis), 7 (Clark), 10, 28; Wikimedia Commons: Tom Head, 23, Wellcome Library, London, 21

Design Elements: Everett Historical/Shutterstock (background map)

Editorial Credits
Editor: Rebecca Felix; Designers: Aruna Rangarajan & Tamara JM Peterson; Production Specialist: Tori Abraham

All internet sites appearing in back matter were available and accurate when this book was sent to press.

EXPLORING THE WEST

In 1803, President Thomas Jefferson purchased 827,000 square miles (2.1 million square kilometers) of land west of the Mississippi River. The Louisiana Purchase doubled the size of the United States.

Jefferson asked explorers Meriwether Lewis and William Clark to lead an official **expedition** in this new land. The 45-person expedition set out from Missouri on May 14, 1804. Over more than two years, the group traveled 8,000 miles (12,900 km). The explorers faced disease, hunger, and other hardships along the way. One person died.

Lewis and Clark mapped western lands. They took notes on unfamiliar animals and plants. Their work helped many Americans head west later.

HOW TO USE THIS BOOK

What if you had explored with the Lewis and Clark expedition? What choices would you have made along the way? Do you think you would have survived?

This book is full of questions that relate to Lewis and Clark's journey. Some are questions real people had to face. The questions are followed by details to help you come to a decision.

Pick one choice or the other. There are no wrong answers! But just like the explorers had to, you should think carefully about your decisions.

Are you ready? Turn the page to pick this or that!

THE LEWIS AND CLARK EXPEDITION

Oregon

Missouri

KEY

Trail

N
W ⊙ E
S

5

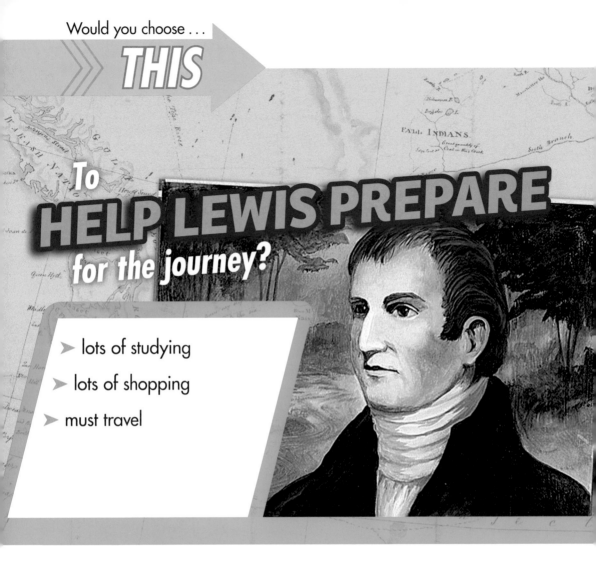

To
HELP LEWIS PREPARE
for the journey?

➤ lots of studying
➤ lots of shopping
➤ must travel

To prepare for the trip, Lewis studied medicine. This involved learning to perform gross medical treatments in practice. One was bloodletting, or making people bleed on purpose. Lewis studied science too. He learned about plants and fossils. He also tackled a big shopping list! Lewis gathered all the supplies for the expedition.

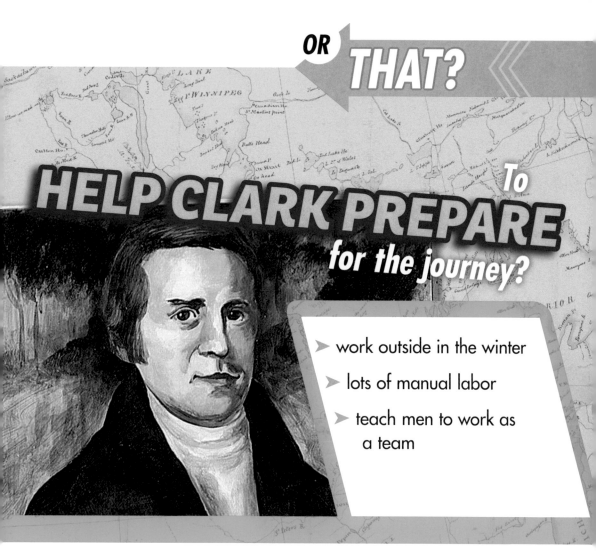

HELP CLARK PREPARE for the journey?

To

➤ work outside in the winter

➤ lots of manual labor

➤ teach men to work as a team

Clark prepared for the journey by finding men to join the team. He trained the men at Camp River Dubois in Illinois. The training took place outdoors in the winter. Clark guided the men through many tasks. This included chopping trees, shooting guns, and loading boats. Sometimes he had to break up fights that occurred between the men.

To LEAVE THE EXPEDITION in April 1805?

- travel on a boat with live animals
- fewer unknown dangers ahead
- miss out on some benefits

In April 1805, a dozen explorers traveled back east. They delivered maps, captured wildlife, and other items to President Jefferson. They watched over live birds, prairie dogs, and more on the journey. Leaving early saved these explorers thousands of miles of travel. However, they lost out on land and money given to explorers who stayed longer.

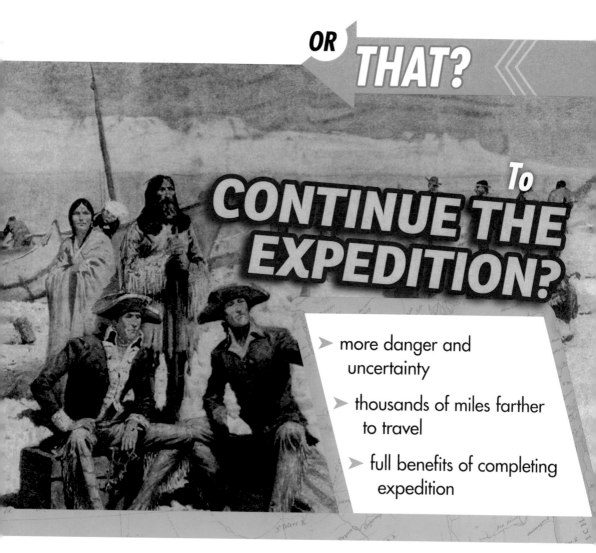

To
CONTINUE THE EXPEDITION?

- more danger and uncertainty
- thousands of miles farther to travel
- full benefits of completing expedition

The rest of the explorers traveled to the Pacific Ocean. They returned to Missouri in September 1806. Continuing meant another long winter in a fort. It also meant another year-and-a-half of traveling. These travelers knew they would face more unknown dangers along the way. However, they earned money, land, and fame for finishing the trip.

Would you choose . . .

THIS

To be a HUNTER?

> could get lost

> have to touch dead animals with bare hands

> danger from weather or accidents

Hunters left the expedition's boats to hunt wild **game** on land. They had to carefully track their movements so they could find the boats later. Those who didn't could get lost in unknown terrain. One hunter was lost for more than two weeks! Hunters sometimes had to hunt in bad weather. In the cold, they could get **frostbite** on their hands, feet, and ears.

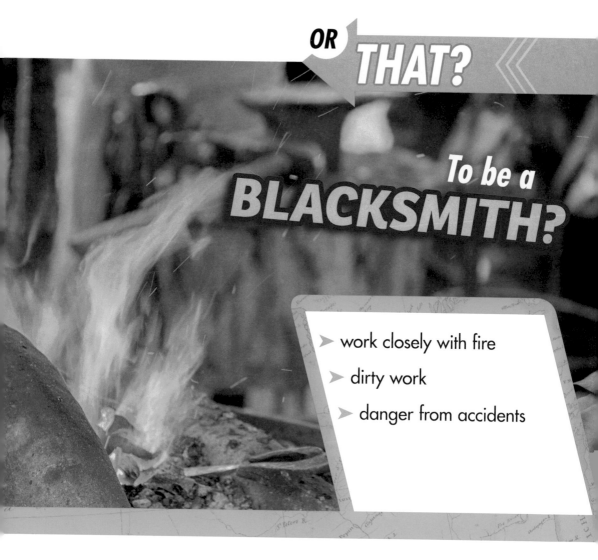

To be a
BLACKSMITH?

> work closely with fire
> dirty work
> danger from accidents

Blacksmiths made axes and knives for the explorers.
This involved bending iron over hot **charcoal** fires.
Blacksmiths cut wood to fuel these fires. Once fueled,
smoke would have made the blacksmiths very dirty.
And they were always at risk of burning themselves
on the fire. Blacksmiths also fixed guns that weren't
working. There was a risk these weapons might
accidentally go off.

Would you choose . . .

THIS

To TRAVEL IN A DUGOUT CANOE?

➤ requires several people to paddle

➤ could tip over if riders don't stay crouched

➤ heavy

Some explorers traveled in dugout canoes. These were made from huge, hollowed-out logs. One empty dugout canoe could weigh up to 1 ton (907 kg)! It required several people to move and paddle it. The explorers had to stay crouched in the canoe to keep it from tipping over. If it did tip, riders could lose their supplies.

To
TRAVEL IN A BULL BOAT?

> light enough for one person to use

> spins when paddled

> could be easily punctured

Explorers also traveled in bull boats. A bull boat was made from buffalo skin stretched over a frame of sticks. It was typically light enough for one person to carry and paddle. However, it spun when paddled. This made it hard to keep on a straight course. The boat's soft skin could also be easily punctured by sticks and rocks. If this happened, the explorer could lose supplies.

THIS

To become sick with
DYSENTERY?

- ➤ from eating spoiled food
- ➤ causes vomiting and diarrhea
- ➤ could die in severe cases

Expedition members likely got dysentery from eating spoiled food. The explorers salted raw meat to make it last longer. But because there were no refrigerators, the meat often spoiled before it dried. Dysentery-causing bacteria would form. People who ate the meat threw up and got **diarrhea**. Dysentery causes death in severe cases.

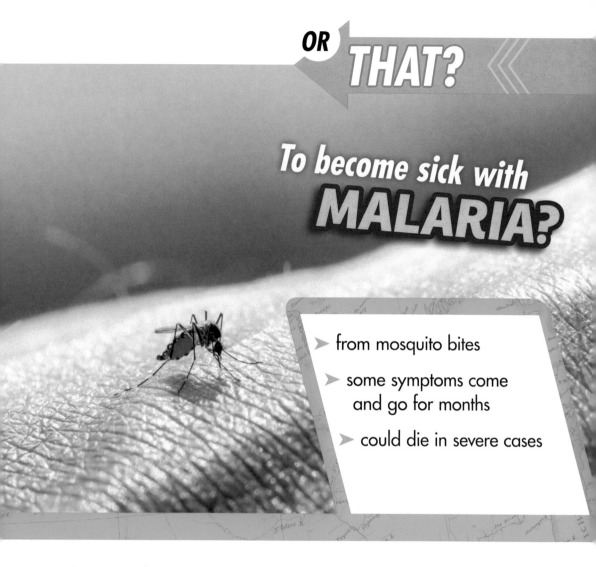

To become sick with
MALARIA?

➤ from mosquito bites

➤ some symptoms come
   and go for months

➤ could die in severe cases

The expedition team sometimes trekked through wet, marshy land. Mosquitoes were common. These blood-sucking bugs could give the explorers diseases such as malaria. Malaria could cause headaches and weakness. It also caused some explorers to experience fevers, sweating, and chills on and off for months. Malaria can be deadly.

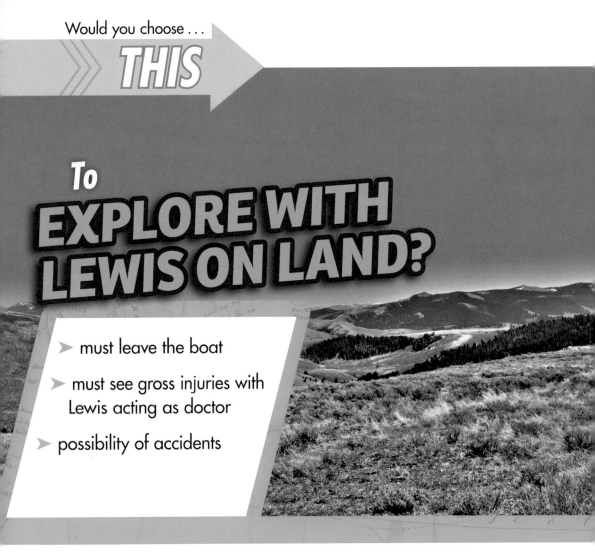

To
EXPLORE WITH LEWIS ON LAND?

➤ must leave the boat

➤ must see gross injuries with Lewis acting as doctor

➤ possibility of accidents

Early in the journey, Lewis often left the boat to collect plants and small animals to send back home. He also supervised hunters. Leaving the boat put Lewis at greater risk of getting lost. He also risked running into wild animals. Lewis was also the group's main doctor. He had to see sickness and accidents up close while helping patients.

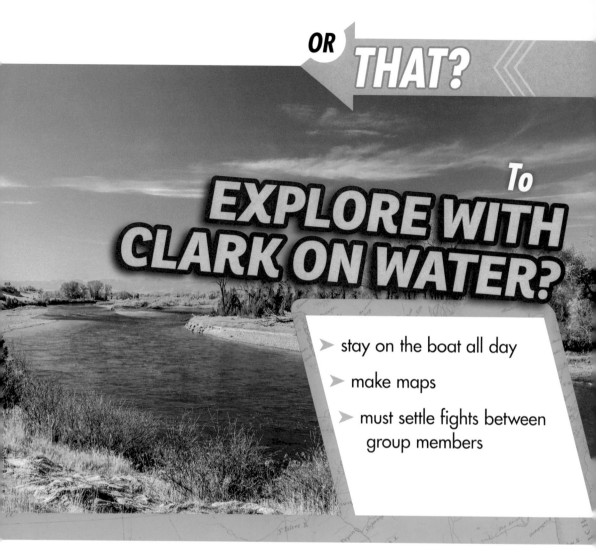

To EXPLORE WITH CLARK ON WATER?

> stay on the boat all day

> make maps

> must settle fights between group members

Clark mostly stayed on the boat during the first part of the journey. This put him at greater risk of falling overboard and drowning in rough waters. Clark was also the main mapmaker. He spent long days making detailed drawings of the land. Because of his military background, Clark was also responsible for settling any fights that broke out.

Would you choose . . .

THIS

To spend a winter at
FORT MANDAN?

- extremely cold temperatures
- dangerous to go outside
- have to touch raw meat

The expedition team spent the winter of 1804–1805 at Fort Mandan in North Dakota. There, temperatures sometimes fell below -45 degrees Fahrenheit (-43 degrees Celsius)! Hunters walked along a frozen river to hunt. The uneven ice blistered their feet. Those inside the fort spent their days slicing and salting raw meat to preserve it.

To spend a winter at FORT CLATSOP?

➤ very rainy

➤ bugs

➤ sickness

Explorers spent the next winter at Fort Clatsop in Oregon. It wasn't as cold there as it was at Fort Mandan. But it was rainy. The explorers spent 106 days at the fort. Only 12 were without rain! The fort also had swarms of fleas that bit the explorers. And the warmer temperatures caused the party's meat to spoil faster. Many people got sick with stomach problems after eating it.

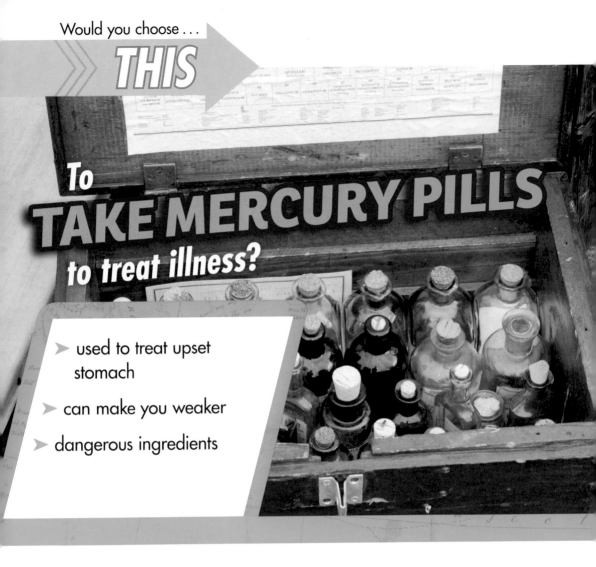

Would you choose . . .

THIS

To **TAKE MERCURY PILLS** to treat illness?

> used to treat upset stomach
> can make you weaker
> dangerous ingredients

Mercury pills were meant to make people throw up and have diarrhea. People thought they would flush out sickness. But explorers actually took the pills to treat diarrhea! The pills made their diarrhea worse. This caused people to lose more fluids. They became weaker instead of getting better.

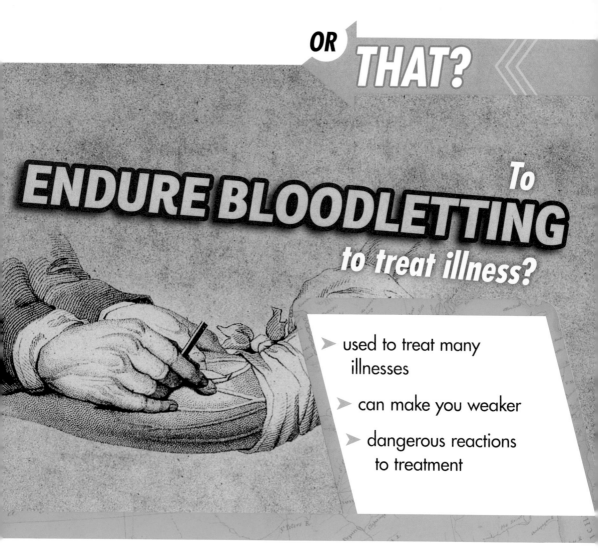

To ENDURE BLOODLETTING to treat illness?

> used to treat many illnesses

> can make you weaker

> dangerous reactions to treatment

In the 1800s, many doctors believed releasing blood from the body helped treat sickness. Lewis and Clark used bloodletting to treat everything from **dehydration** to chest infections among their crew. They used a knife to pierce the skin. Blood collected in a bowl below. The treatment did not help anyone get better. Instead, it likely caused further weakness.

To eat

PORTABLE SOUP?

- ➤ only eaten when there are no other food options
- ➤ doesn't taste good
- ➤ unappetizing texture

Lewis brought 193 pounds (88 kg) of "portable soup" to eat when game was scarce. The soup was dehydrated. It looked like dried brown jelly. When boiled in water, the jelly became liquid. Many expedition members thought the soup had a texture like thick glue. Once, the explorers chose to eat a horse instead of eating the soup.

To eat
BOUDIN BLANC?

> must hunt for it

> taste enjoyed by explorers

> possibility of eating
undigested buffalo food

Boudin blanc is sausage made by stuffing a buffalo
intestine. When hunters shot buffalo, carrying the meat
required many men. Then, they packed its intestine
with shoulder and kidney meat from a buffalo or deer.
Whatever was in the buffalo's gut was pushed out to make
room for the meat. So, it was possible you'd be eating
little pieces of whatever the buffalo had been **digesting**.

23

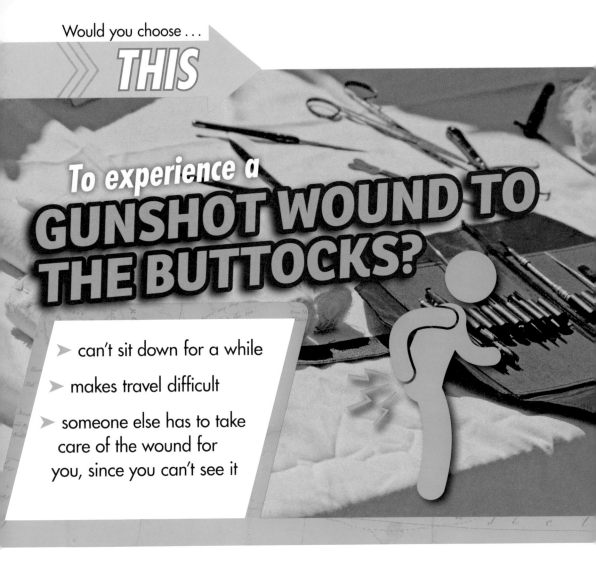

To experience a

GUNSHOT WOUND TO THE BUTTOCKS?

- ➤ can't sit down for a while

- ➤ makes travel difficult

- ➤ someone else has to take care of the wound for you, since you can't see it

Gunshot accidents could happen during hunting trips. Lewis was accidentally shot in the buttocks during the expedition! Getting shot in the butt meant you wouldn't be able to sit down for a week or more. You would have to lie facedown. Even after the injury healed, you would have pain and stiffness for weeks.

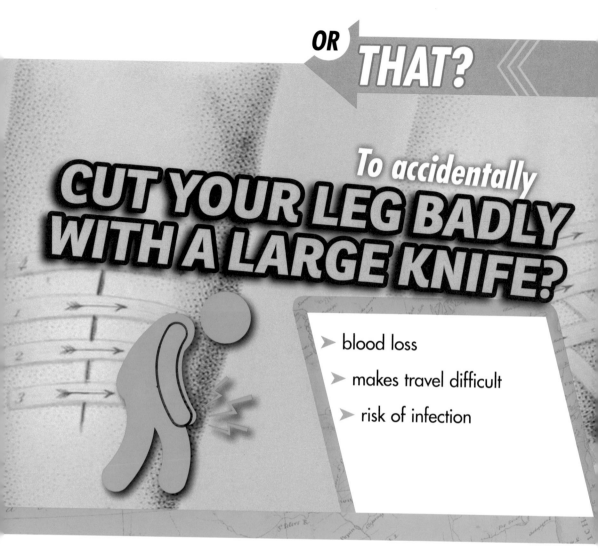

To accidentally **CUT YOUR LEG BADLY WITH A LARGE KNIFE?**

➤ blood loss

➤ makes travel difficult

➤ risk of infection

Knife accidents could also happen while hunting. A leg wound would be painful. It would also cause you to lose lots of blood, which could make you weak. You might be able to move afterward. But everyday activities would be difficult for weeks. For example, the cut may rub against a horse when riding, causing pain.

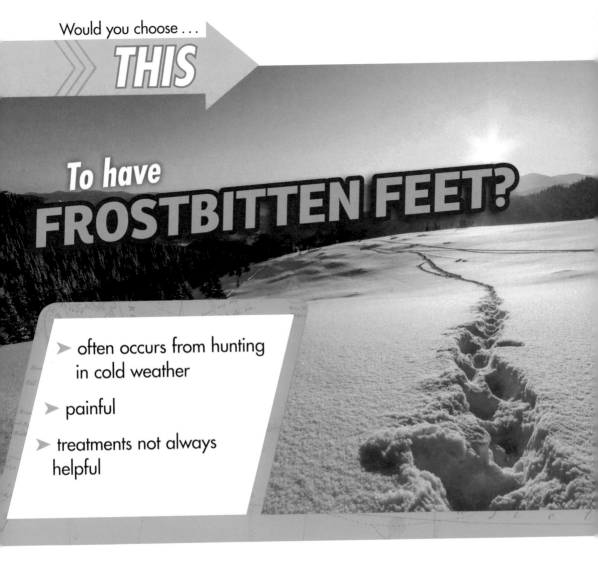

THIS

To have FROSTBITTEN FEET?

- often occurs from hunting in cold weather
- painful
- treatments not always helpful

Explorers had to hunt in freezing winter weather. Some got frostbite on their toes. Frostbite makes the affected body parts sting and then go numb. At the time, foot frostbite was treated by soaking the toes in cold water. But this could cause more harm. In bad cases, frostbite can lead to **amputation** of toes or an entire foot.

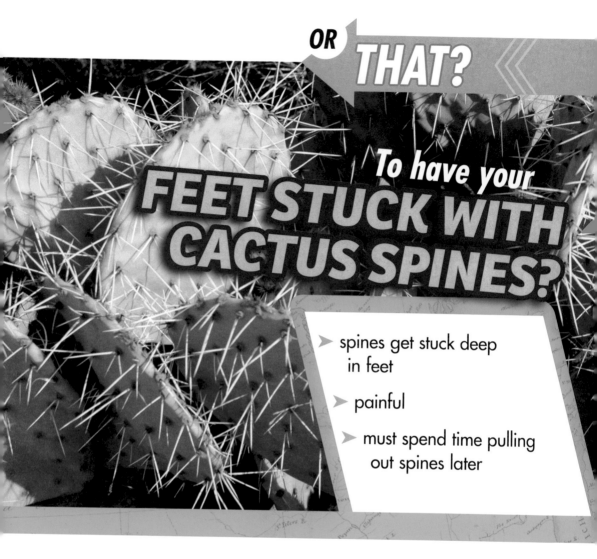

To have your
FEET STUCK WITH CACTUS SPINES?

> spines get stuck deep in feet

> painful

> must spend time pulling out spines later

The explorers wore soft shoes called moccasins. These did not protect their feet from cactus spines in the desert. The spines caused people's feet to swell and ache. The pain could make it hard to walk. At night, the explorers pulled out any spines still in their feet. Lewis pulled out 17 cactus spines in one sitting!

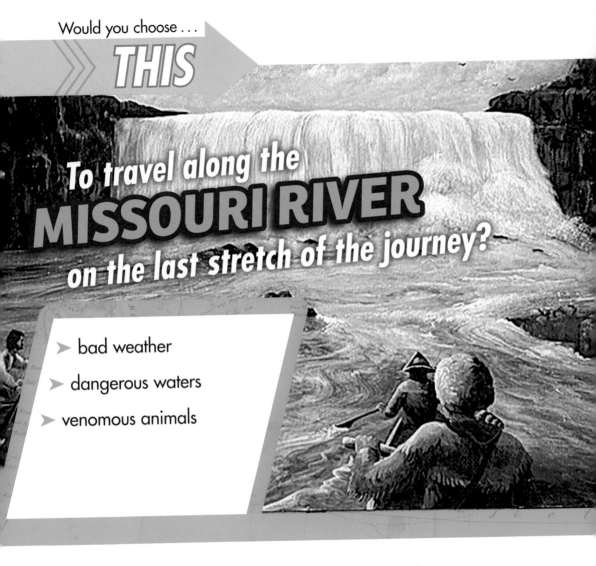

To travel along the

MISSOURI RIVER

on the last stretch of the journey?

- bad weather
- dangerous waters
- venomous animals

The expedition split near the end of the journey. Lewis went down the Missouri River. Several men joined him. Heavy rains made the river move quickly and become more dangerous. People and supplies were at risk of being washed overboard. The group also had a run-in with a rattlesnake. This snake's **venom** can kill people.

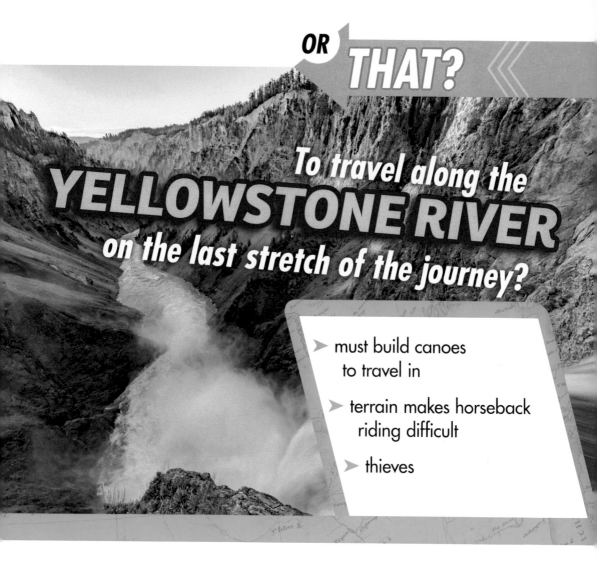

To travel along the
YELLOWSTONE RIVER
on the last stretch of the journey?

> must build canoes to travel in

> terrain makes horseback riding difficult

> thieves

Clark traveled along the Yellowstone River with several expedition members at the end of the journey. They rode on horseback to reach the river. The land was rocky and hard to ride on. After one man fell off his horse, the group looked for trees to make canoes. While making the boats, **thieves** stole half the group's horses.

LIGHTNING ROUND

Would you choose to . . .

➤ fight off a buffalo or a grizzly bear charging through your camp?

➤ fall out of a boat or fall off of a horse?

➤ eat beaver or wolf meat for dinner?

➤ face a cloud of fleas or mosquitoes?

➤ see a prairie dog colony or a beached whale?

➤ eat dog meat or horse meat when food is scarce?

➤ be a carpenter who builds boats or a boatman who steers them?

➤ trade with American Indians for horses or food?

GLOSSARY

amputation (AM-pyuh-tay-shun)—the process of having a limb cut off, usually because it is diseased or damaged

charcoal (CHAR-kohl)—a substance made from incompletely burned wood

dehydration (dee-HYE-dray-shun)—lacking enough water in your body for normal functioning

diarrhea (dye-uh-REE-uh)—a condition in which normally solid waste from your body becomes liquid

digest (DYE-jest)—to break down food in the body so it can be absorbed and used for energy

expedition (ek-spuh-DISH-uhn)—a long trip made for a specific purpose

frostbite (FRAWST-bite)—a condition that occurs when extremely cold temperatures damage parts of a person's body

game (GAME)—wild animals hunted for sport or food

interpreter (in-TUR-prit-ur)—a person who translates a conversation between two people who speak different languages

intestine (in-TES-tin)—a long tube in the body that digests food and absorbs liquids and salts

thief (THEEF)—a person who steals others' belongings or money

venom (VEN-uhm)—poison produced by certain animals, including some species of spiders and snakes

vomit (VAH-mit)—to bring up food from the stomach and expel it through the mouth

READ MORE

Davis, Hasan. *The Journey of York: The Unsung Hero of the Lewis and Clark Expedition*. North Mankato, MN: Capstone Editions, 2019.

Lawrence, Blythe. *The Lewis and Clark Expedition*. New York: AV2 by Weigl, 2020.

Murray, Laura K. *Sacagawea*. North Mankato, MN: Pebble, 2020.

INTERNET SITES

DK Find Out—Lewis and Clark
https://www.dkfindout.com/us/history/explorers
/lewis-and-clark/

Ducksters—Biography: Lewis and Clark
https://www.ducksters.com/biography/explorers
/lewis_and_clark.php

National Geographic Kids—America Heads West
https://kids.nationalgeographic.com/explore/history
/lewis-and-clark/